Fun and Festive

FALL CRAFTS

Leaf Rubbings, Dancing Scarecrows, and Pinecone Turkeys

Randel McGee

Enslow Elementary
an imprint of

Enslow Publishers, Inc.
40 Industrial Road
Box 398
Berkeley Heights, NJ 07922
USA

www.enslow.com

Dedicated to Lia and Caitlynn McGee

Enslow Elementary, an imprint of Enslow Publishers, Inc.

Enslow Elementary® is a registered trademark of Enslow Publishers, Inc.

Library of Congress Cataloging-in-Publication Data

McGee, Randel.
    Fun and festive fall crafts : leaf rubbings, dancing scarecrows, and pinecone turkeys / Randel McGee.
        pages cm — (Fun and festive crafts for the seasons)
    Includes bibliographical references and index.
    Summary: "Includes the scientific explanation behind the autumn season, a related myth, and step-by-step
        instructions on how to make eight fall-themed crafts out of various materials"— Provided by publisher.
    Audience: Grades 4 to 6.
    ISBN 978-0-7660-4320-6
    1. Handicraft—Juvenile literature. 2. Autumn—Juvenile literature. I. Title.
    TT160.M3847 2014
    745.5—dc23
                                           2013039203

Future editions:
Paperback ISBN: 978-1-4644-0585-3
Single-User PDF ISBN: 978-1-4646-1282-4

EPUB ISBN: 978-1-4645-1282-7
Multi-User PDF ISBN: 978-0-7660-5914-6

Printed in the United States of America

052014 Lake Book Manufacturing, Inc., Melrose Park, IL

10 9 8 7 6 5 4 3 2 1

To Our Readers: We have done our best to make sure all Internet addresses in this book were active and appropriate when we went to press. However, the author and the publisher have no control over and assume no liability for the material available on those Internet sites or on other Web sites they may link to. Any comments or suggestions can be sent by e-mail to comments@enslow.com or to the address on the back cover.

Every effort has been made to locate all copyright holders of material used in this book. If any errors or omissions have occurred, corrections will be made in future editions of this book.

♻ Enslow Publishers, Inc., is committed to printing our books on recycled paper. The paper in every book contains 10% to 30% post-consumer waste (PCW). The cover board on the outside of each book contains 100% PCW. Our goal is to do our part to help young people and the environment too!

Photo Credits: Crafts prepared by Randel McGee and p. 48; craft photography by Enslow Publishers, Inc.; Designua/Shutterstock.com, p. 5.

Cover photo: Crafts prepared by Randel McGee; photography by Enslow Publishers, Inc.

Contents

AUTHOR'S NOTE: The projects in this book were created for this particular season. However, I invite readers to be imaginative and find new ways to use the ideas in this book to create different projects of their own. Please feel free to share pictures of your work with me through www.mcgeeproductions.com. Happy crafting!

FALL!

Legends say that in ancient China, there were ten suns that took turns warming Earth. One day, all the suns came up at the same time. They burned Earth! The crops started to die, and the rivers began to dry up. Hou Yi (How Yee) was the best archer in all of China. His wife, Chang E (Chahng Eh), asked him to save their crops. Hou Yi ran to a mountain and shot nine of the suns out of the sky. The crops were saved!

The Emperor of the Sky rewarded Hou Yi with a potion that would make him and Chang E live forever. They decided to drink the potion in the light of the first full moon after the harvest. On that day, Hou Yi went hunting. While he was away, his evil neighbor broke into his house to steal the potion for himself. Chang E drank the potion rather than let the wicked man have it.

Hou Yi returned in time to see his wife floating into the sky as an immortal. She stayed on the moon. When the moon was full after the harvest, Chang E danced and waved to her husband back on Earth. Hou Yi lit a special lantern so she could see him, and he sent her a round moon cake tied to an arrow. Chinese people all over the world celebrate the Moon Festival at harvesttime and light fancy lanterns and serve round moon cakes.

In the Northern Hemisphere, autumn is the time of year when Earth begins to tilt farther away from the sun. The days grow shorter and the nights grow colder. The autumnal equinox is the day that the hours of daylight and night are the same. This usually happens around September 22.

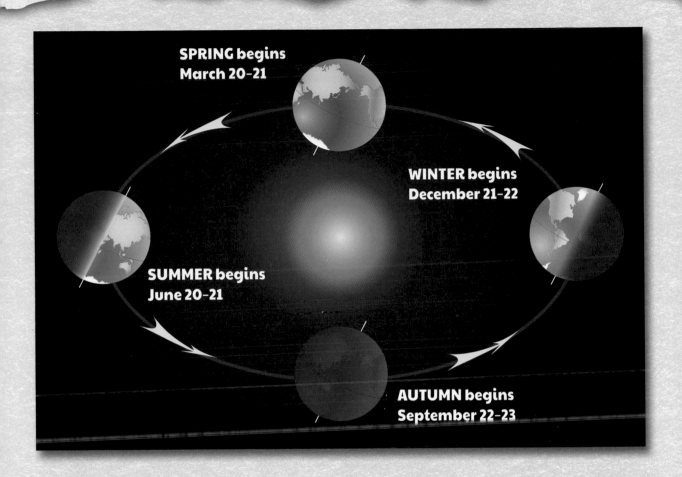

SPRING begins
March 20-21

WINTER begins
December 21-22

SUMMER begins
June 20-21

AUTUMN begins
September 22-23

Tree leaves change from green to yellow, orange, red, and brown, and the school year begins again. English-speaking people often call this time *fall* from an old phrase, "Fall of the Leaf," that described what happened to the trees. There are holidays to celebrate the harvest all around the world, such as the Moon Festival in China, Halloween in Ireland and the United States, and Thanksgiving in North America. The crafts in this book give you some projects you can take back to school with you. Enjoy the changing season!

Leaf Rubbings

During the spring and summer months, the leaves make chlorophyll (KLOR-o-fill), a green food that helps the tree grow. When the days get shorter and the nights get colder, the leaves stop making chlorophyll. Without chlorophyll, the green color fades away showing the real color of the leaf: yellow, red, orange, or brown. Then the leaves dry up and fall off.

What You Will Need:

- freshly fallen leaves
- paper towels
- sheets of newsprint, butcher paper, or bulletin board paper
- crayons
- scissors
- glue
- construction paper or poster board

WHAT TO DO:

1. Gently rinse the leaves with water and dry them with the paper towels.

2. Lay the leaves on a smooth flat surface such as a table or desk.

#2

3. Cover the leaves with a sheet of newsprint, butcher paper, or bulletin board paper.

4. Remove some of the paper wrapping from the crayon so that you can use the side rather than the point. **Note:** There are large crayons that have flat sides and work well for this project.

5. Use the side of the crayon to gently rub the paper covering the leaves until you see the shape of the leaves.

#5

6. Use scissors to trim or shape the edge of the paper with the leaf rubbings as you wish.

7. Glue the leaf rubbings to a sheet of construction paper or poster board.

8. Use the mounted rubbing as a wall decoration or place mat.

#7

PENCIL PAL

In 1500, a mineral was found in England that was black and soft and left a mark. The English were soon selling thin rods of the mineral to use for writing and drawing. They called it graphite (GRAFF-ite). William Monroe was the first American to put the graphite into a wooden holder and make a pencil like people use today. Put pizzazz on your pencil with playful pencil pals!

WHAT YOU WILL NEED:

- scissors
- pencils (one for the project and another to draw with)
- craft foam—any color
- hole punch

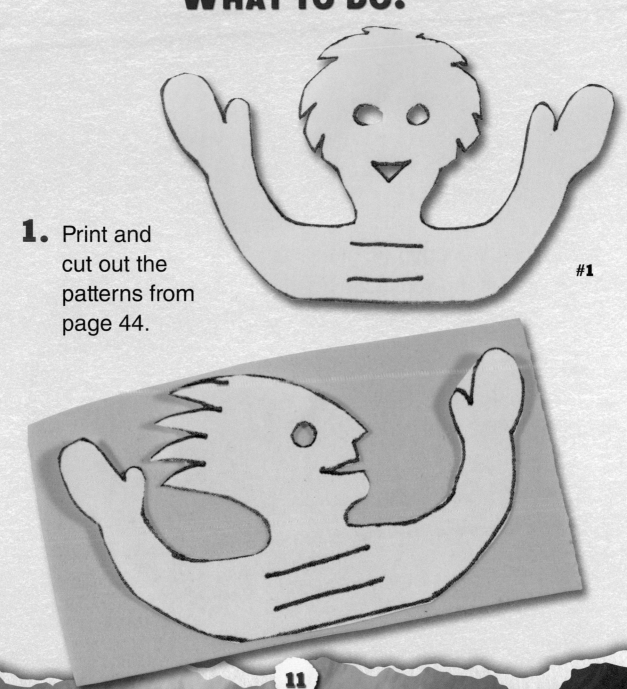

#1

1. Print and cut out the patterns from page 44.

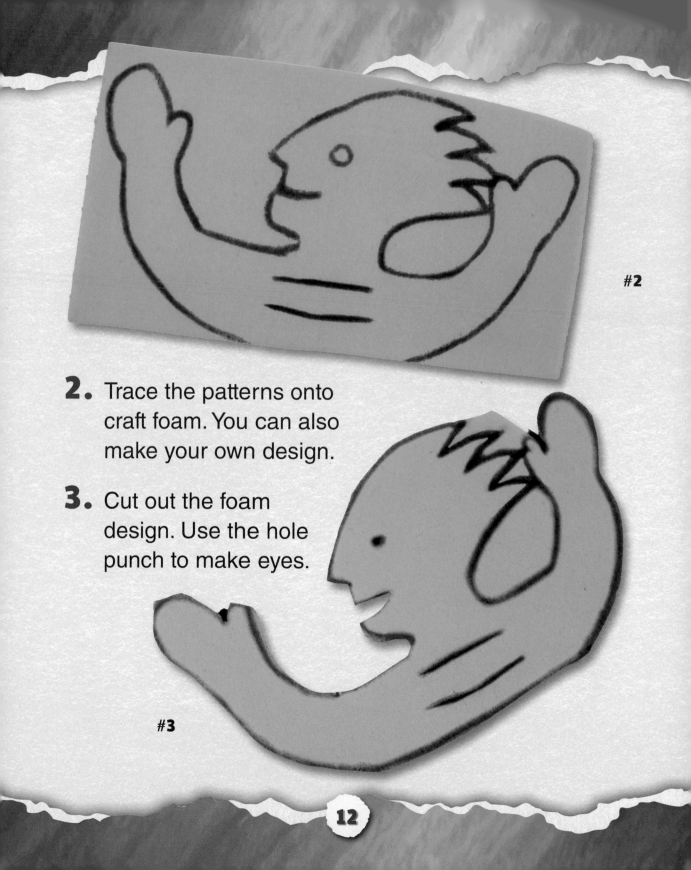

#2

2. Trace the patterns onto craft foam. You can also make your own design.

3. Cut out the foam design. Use the hole punch to make eyes.

#3

4. Slip the eraser end of the pencil through the two slits on the body of the pencil pal. Your pencil pal is now ready to join you for a busy day!

#4

"KNOWLEDGE IS POWER" BOOK PROTECTOR

Early books were made from clay tablets, metal plates, thin wooden boards, and long sheets of papyrus made from crushed plant stems and bark. Most early books were considered treasures and were protected from dirt and damage by special boxes or coverings. Francis Bacon, an English author and philosopher (1561–1626), was so impressed with the things he learned from books that he wrote the famous line: "Knowledge is power." Protect the power source! Decorate your schoolbooks and storybooks with these covers.

WHAT YOU WILL NEED:

- brown paper grocery bag
- scissors
- pencil
- ruler
- construction paper— different colors
- glue
- permanent markers

WHAT TO DO:

1. Cut off the bottom of the brown paper bag and cut along one corner to open the bag out into a single sheet.

#1

2. Lay the paper out flat on a smooth work area such as a desk or table. Gently open the book you are covering on the paper with the pages facing up.

3. Measure out from the book between 1 and 2 inches, depending on how big the book is, and make marks on the paper with a pencil. Use a ruler to connect those marks with straight lines. You now have a large rectangle.

4. Set the book aside for a minute. Cut out the large rectangle.

5. Lay the open book on the cut sheet of paper so that it fits evenly from top to bottom and side to side. Draw a line along the paper near all four edges of the book. **Note:** Be careful not to mark the book.

#5

6. Set the book aside again. Fold the long sides along the pencil lines, top and bottom, then fold in both of the sides. This will make a sort of pocket on each side of the paper.

#7

7. Slip the outside edge of the book cover into the pockets on both sides. Gently close the book and crease the edges of the book cover to fit.

8. Use construction paper and markers to make the power images on page 43. Glue them onto the cover. Let dry.

#8

BIRDIE BOOKMARK

Ever since books were created, people have used bookmarks to show them where they stopped reading. During the time of Queen Victoria (1837–1901), English girls were taught how to embroider by making pretty bookmarks. In modern times, you can find bookmarks made of metal, magnets, wood, bone, paper, plastic, and craft foam. Hurry and make one so that you do not lose your place in this book!

WHAT YOU WILL NEED:

- scissors
- craft foam—different colors
- pencil
- glue
- permanent markers

1. Print and cut out the pattern from page 39. Trace the pattern onto craft foam.

#1

2. Cut the design out of the craft foam.

#2

3. Decorate the bookmark with pieces of craft foam, glue, and permanent markers as you wish. Let the glue dry.

#3

4. Gently bend back the top of the birdie and slide the beak and wings over the page you want to mark. The body goes behind the page.

#4

ay have had ʰe wild turkey to eat, but t o would
(deer meat) ducks, geese, lobsters, oysters, fish, beans, c
and corn pudding. They did not celebrate a day of Thar
time ever

Bat Marionette

Bats are often used in decorations for Halloween. The Irish of long ago thought that bats must be evil spirits because they would fly around the bonfires that people lit on Halloween night to chase away evil spirits. The fires would attract flying insects and the bats would swoop in to eat the insects. You can make this bat marionette swoop around and flap its wings.

What you will need:

- scissors
- black craft foam
- pencil
- pliers
- a wire coat hanger
- duct tape
- craft sticks—one large and one small
- modeling material
- watercolors or poster paints and paintbrush
- craft eyes or beads
- glue

WHAT TO DO:

1. Print and cut out the patterns from page 44. Trace the patterns onto black craft foam and cut them out.

#1

2. **Have an adult** use the pliers to unwind and straighten out a thin wire coat hanger. Use the pliers to trim off the twisted ends. Make a wire about 18 inches long.

3. Bend 1 inch of one end of the wire like an "L." At the other end, bend 4 inches of the wire the opposite way.

#3

4. Use the duct tape to attach the large craft stick to the 4-inch-length of wire to make a handle. Wrap the handle with the duct tape once or twice.

#4

5. Make two balls of modeling material, one about the size of a plum and the other the size of a cherry.

#5

6. Push the 1-inch length of wire into the larger ball and shape it for the body. Attach the smaller ball of material as the head. Use the smaller craft stick to make grooves in the body and head for the wings, tail, and ears. Let the modeling material dry overnight.

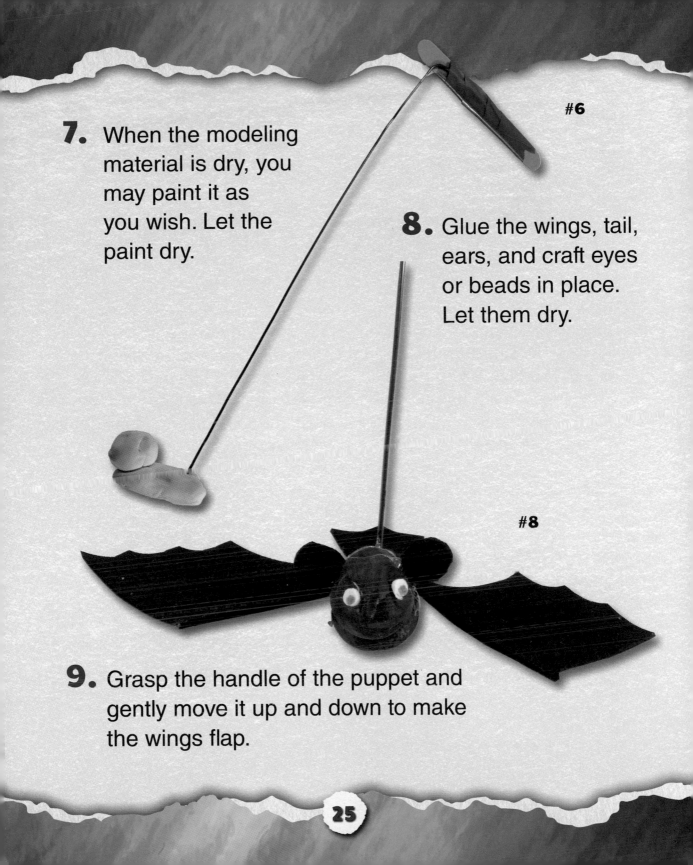

7. When the modeling material is dry, you may paint it as you wish. Let the paint dry.

#6

8. Glue the wings, tail, ears, and craft eyes or beads in place. Let them dry.

#8

9. Grasp the handle of the puppet and gently move it up and down to make the wings flap.

POTATO STAMP PLACE MAT

When Spanish explorers met the American Indian tribes of South America, they found them eating a root they had never seen before. Some of the native people called the root *papa* and others called it *batata*. The Spanish mixed the sounds and called it *patata*, which is where we get the English word *potato*. A potato can be used in many ways. You can bake it, boil it, fry it, mash it . . . and make stamped designs with it! ASK AN ADULT to help you cut the potatoes and carve the designs. You can use the designs for place mats or other decorations for harvest festivals or Thanksgiving Day meals.

WHAT YOU WILL NEED:

- a fresh potato
- a kitchen knife
- acrylic paints, watercolors, or poster paints
- paintbrush
- construction paper— various colors

WHAT TO DO:

1. **Have an adult** slice the potato in half with the knife. **Note:** Serrated knives may leave lines in the stamped designs.

2. Use some of the designs from page 41 as guides for your potato stamps, or make some of your own.

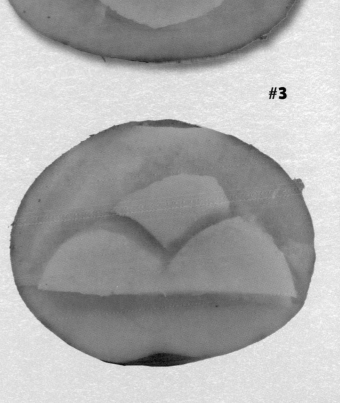

#3

3. The adult can cut the design into the flat part of the sliced potato. Carefully cut away pieces of the potato that are not part of the design. **Note:** The design should stick up about ¼ inch from the rest of the potato.

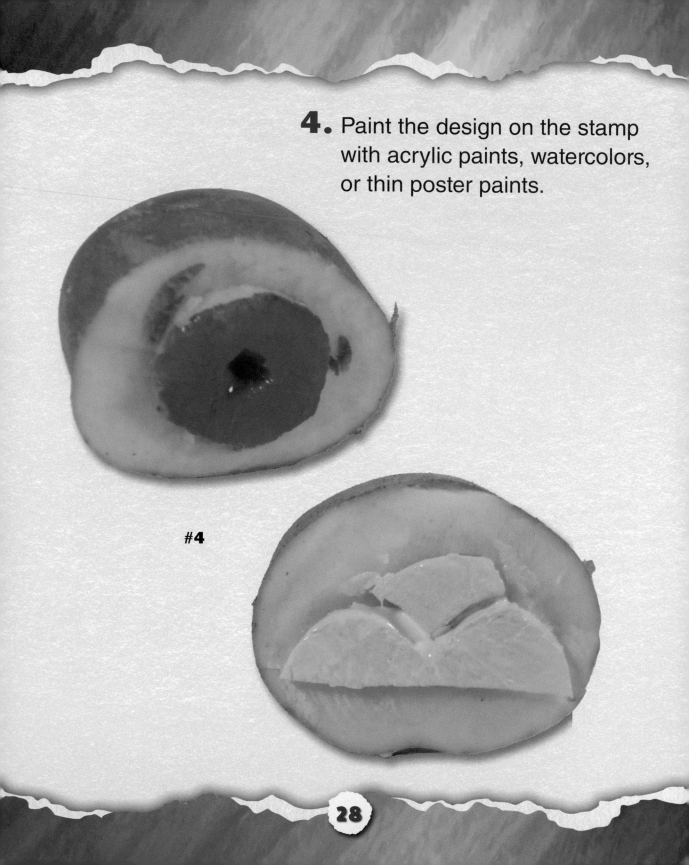

4. Paint the design on the stamp with acrylic paints, watercolors, or thin poster paints.

#4

5. While the paint is still wet, stamp the design on construction paper. Make a pattern using two or more designs as you wish. Brush more paint on the stamp as needed. **Note:** Do not let too much paint stay around the edges of the design. That will cause the designs to smear.

6. After you are done stamping, let the paint dry.

7. Use the stamp designs on decorations and place mats.

#6

PINECONE TURKEY

The Europeans who first came to America thought that the turkey was like a guinea fowl, a large bird from Africa. The guinea fowl was also called a Turkey fowl because it was brought to Europe on ships from Turkey. When a male turkey wants to show how big and strong he is, he makes his feathers rise up, and he spreads his tail feathers like a fan. The turkey in this project is showing off as your Thanksgiving decoration.

WHAT YOU WILL NEED:

- a pinecone—one that has dried and opened is best
- long-bristled cleaning brush or old paintbrush
- scissors
- pencil
- construction paper or craft foam—different colors
- hole punch
- pipe cleaners—red or gray
- glue
- crayons (optional)

WHAT TO DO:

1. Clean the pinecone with the brush. **Be careful** as some pinecones have sharp spines.

#1

2. Print and cut out the patterns from page 40 for the tail, wings, wattle, feet, and beak. Trace them onto the construction paper or craft foam. The tail and wings can be brown, the wattle can be red, and the feet and beak can be orange, or choose colors as you wish. Use a hole punch to make two dark, round eyes for the turkey.

#2

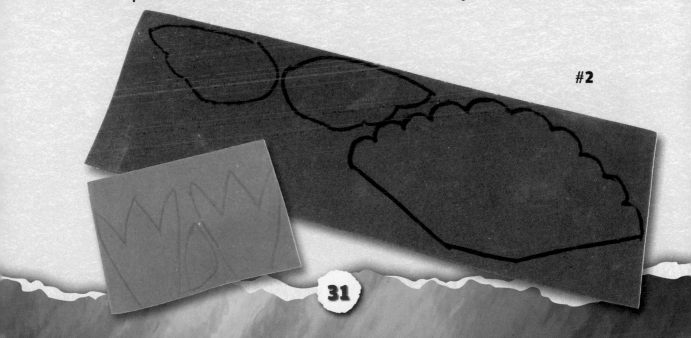

3. Cut out the pattern pieces. **Note:** You may have to change the size of the pattern a little to fit the size of the pinecone.

4. Shape the pipe cleaner into the neck and head of the turkey.

#4

5. Glue the beak, wattle, and eyes to the pipe cleaner head. Decorate the tail with pieces of construction paper, craft foam, or crayons. Let the glue dry.

#5

6. Glue the neck and head of the turkey to the small end of the pinecone. Glue the wings onto the sides of the pinecone. Glue the tail sticking up at the large end of the pinecone. Glue the feet underneath the turkey. Let the glue dry.

#6

7. If you wish, glue the turkey onto a construction paper base.

#7

BARN-DANCE SCARECROW

Farmers around the world have always had the same problem: keeping crows and other birds and animals away from their crops. Japanese farmers made straw statues of people with bows and arrows to frighten away animals from their fields. These were some of the first scarecrows. Scarecrows have become symbols of farms and harvesttime.

WHAT YOU WILL NEED:

- a cereal box (or similar lightweight cardboard container)
- construction paper—different colors
- glue
- scissors
- pencil
- crayons or markers
- lightweight cardboard
- hole punch
- yarn or twine
- tape or a hot glue gun (optional)
- brass paper fastener
- plastic drinking straw

WHAT TO DO:

1. Cover the cereal box with red or brown construction paper. Keep the paper in place with glue. This will be the barn. Let the glue dry.

2. Print and cut out the barn pattern from page 42. Trace it onto the front and back of the cereal box.

3. Cut along the solid black lines to form the top of the barn and on one side of the cereal box to make the barn doors. Decorate the barn with crayons or markers.

4. Print and cut out the scarecrow patterns from page 42. Trace them onto lightweight cardboard. Color them as you wish.

#2

#3

#4

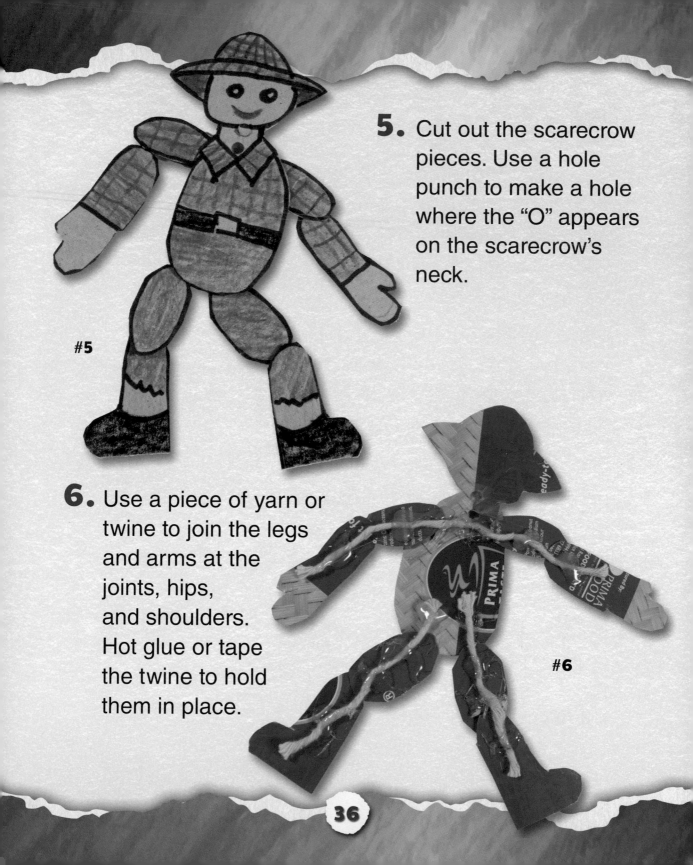

5. Cut out the scarecrow pieces. Use a hole punch to make a hole where the "O" appears on the scarecrow's neck.

#5

6. Use a piece of yarn or twine to join the legs and arms at the joints, hips, and shoulders. Hot glue or tape the twine to hold them in place.

#6

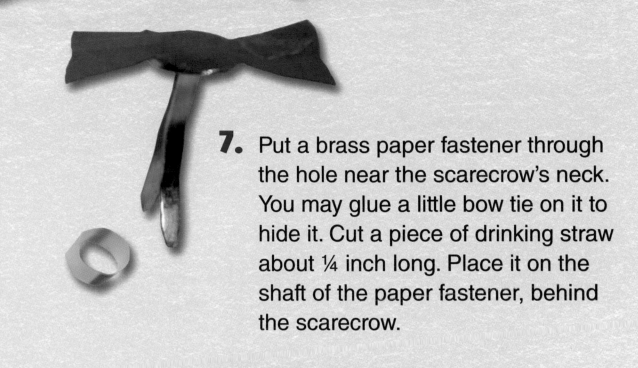

7. Put a brass paper fastener through the hole near the scarecrow's neck. You may glue a little bow tie on it to hide it. Cut a piece of drinking straw about ¼ inch long. Place it on the shaft of the paper fastener, behind the scarecrow.

#7

8. Open the barn doors and poke a hole through the back wall. Put the point of the paper fastener through the hole. Set the pointed end of the fastener in place on the outside of the barn. When you open the barn doors and shake the barn gently from side to side, the scarecrow will dance and shimmy.

#8

PATTERNS

The percentages included on the patterns tell you how much to enlarge or shrink the image using a copier. Most copiers and printers have an adjustable size/percentage feature to change the size of an image when you print it. After you print the pattern to its correct size, cut it out. Trace it onto the material listed in the craft.

Birdie Bookmark

Shrink to 80%

Pinecone Turkey Parts

Enlarge to 135%

Wattle

**Beak
(fold on dotted line)**

**Wing
(make 2)**

**Foot
(make 2)**

Tail

Symbols for Potato Stamps

Size depends on potato

Tepee

Arrowhead

Cloud   **Turkey track**   **Sun**

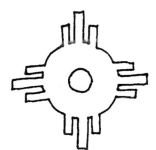

Snow cloud   **Deer track**   **Squash blossom**

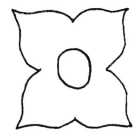

Barn-Dance Scarecrow

Arm
(make 2)

Leg
(make 2)

Size depends on box used

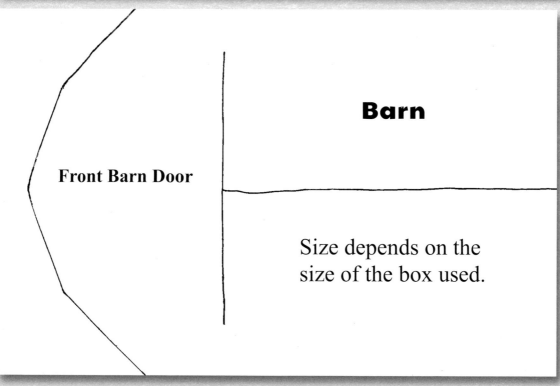

Barn

Front Barn Door

Size depends on the
size of the box used.

"Knowledge Is Power" Book Protectors

Enlarge/shrink as needed to fit cover

Pencil Pals

Enlarge to 140%

Bat Marionette

At 100%

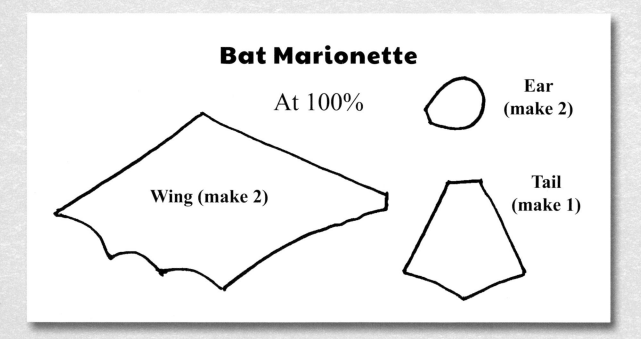

Ear
(make 2)

Wing (make 2)

Tail
(make 1)

READ ABOUT

Books

Berger, Thomas, and Petra Berger. *Crafts Through the Year*. Edinburgh, Scotland: Floris Books, 2011.

Lim, Annalees. *10 Minute Crafts forAutumn*. London: Wayland Publishers Ltd., 2014.

Ross, Kathy. *Step-by-Step Crafts for Fall*. Honesdale, Penn.: Boyds Mills Press, 2006.

Internet Addresses

Spoonful: Fall Crafts and Printables

http://spoonful.com/autumn/fall-crafts

DLTK's Crafts for Kids: Easy Autumn Crafts

http://www.dltk-kids.com/crafts/fall/

Visit Randel McGee's Web site at

http://www.mcgeeproductions.com

INDEX

ABOUT THE AUTHOR

Randel McGee has liked to make things and has played with paper and scissors as long as he can remember. He also likes telling stories and performing. He is an internationally recognized storyteller, ventriloquist, and puppeteer. He and his dragon puppet, Groark, have performed all around the United States and Asia and have appeared in two award-winning video series on character education. He also portrays the famous author Hans Christian Andersen in storytelling performances, where he makes amazing cut-paper designs while he tells stories, just like Andersen did. He likes showing teachers and children the fun they can have with paper projects, storytelling, and puppetry. Randel McGee lives in central California with his wife, Marsha. They have five grown children.